D1064792

Countries We Come From

Morocco

by Joyce Markovics

Consultant: Marjorie Faulstich Orellana, PhD
Professor of Urban Schooling
University of California, Los Angeles

BEARPORT
PUBLISHING

New York, New York

Credits

Cover, © Poike/iStock and © Olena Z/Shutterstock; TOC, © benhammad/Shutterstock; 4, © Vixit/Shutterstock; 5L, © hadynyah/iStock; 5R, © hadynyah/iStock; 7, © posztos/Shutterstock; 8, © Karol Koziowski/AGE Fotostock; 9T, © monticello/iStock; 9B, © longtaildog/Shutterstock; 10LT, © reptiles4all/Shutterstock; 10LB, © bulinko/Shutterstock; 10–11, © Yavuz Sariyildiz/Shutterstock; 12, © John Copland/Shutterstock; 13T, © Album/Alamy; 13B, © Christian Liewig/ABACA/Newscom; 14, © Matyas Rehak/Shutterstock; 15, © canyalcin/Shutterstock; 16, © wanderluster/iStock; 17, © Andrzej Kubik/Shutterstock; 18, © Madrugada Verde/Shutterstock; 19, © AlejandroCarnicero/Shutterstock; 20L, © Monique Loman/Shutterstock; 20–21, © narvikk/iStock; 22T, © Chris Caldicott/Axiom Photography/AGE Fotostock; 22B, © Elinecicka/Shutterstock; 23, © ArdenSt/iStock; 24, © Press750/Dreamstime; 25T, © Jacques Sierpinski/Hemis/AGE Fotostock; 25B, © Klemen K. Misic/Shutterstock; 26, © hadynyah/iStock; 27T, © Maurizio De Mattei/Shutterstock; 27B, © haraldmuc/Shutterstock; 28L, © EhayDy/Shutterstock; 28–29, © Elzbieta Sekowska/Shutterstock; 30T, © Phillip Lange/Shutterstock and © Andrey Lobachev/Shutterstock; 30B, © AlxeyPnferov/iStock; 31 (T to B), © uchar/iStock, © canyalcin/Shutterstock, © Geoffrey Newland/Shutterstock, and © ikoneo/Shutterstock; 32, © Lefteris Papaulakis/Shutterstock.

Publisher: Kenn Goin
Senior Editor: Joyce Tavolacci
Creative Director: Spencer Brinker
Design: Debrah Kaiser
Photo Researcher: Thomas Persano

Library of Congress Cataloging-in-Publication Data

Names: Markovics, Joyce L., author.
Title: Morocco / by Joyce Markovics.
Description: New York : Bearport Publishing Company, Inc., 2020. | Series: Countries we come from
Identifiers: LCCN 2019007135 (print) | LCCN 2019007423 (ebook) | ISBN 9781642805864 (ebook) | ISBN 9781642805321 (library)
Subjects: LCSH: Morocco—Juvenile literature.
Classification: LCC DT305 (ebook) | LCC DT305 .M347 2020 (print) | DDC 964—dc23
LC record available at https://lccn.loc.gov/2019007135

For more information, write to Bearport Publishing Company, Inc., 45 West 21st Street, Suite 3B, New York, New York 10010. Printed in the United States of America.

10 9 8 7 6 5 4 3 2 1

Contents

This Is Morocco

BOLD

Welcoming

DRY

Morocco is located in North Africa. This country is about the same size as California.

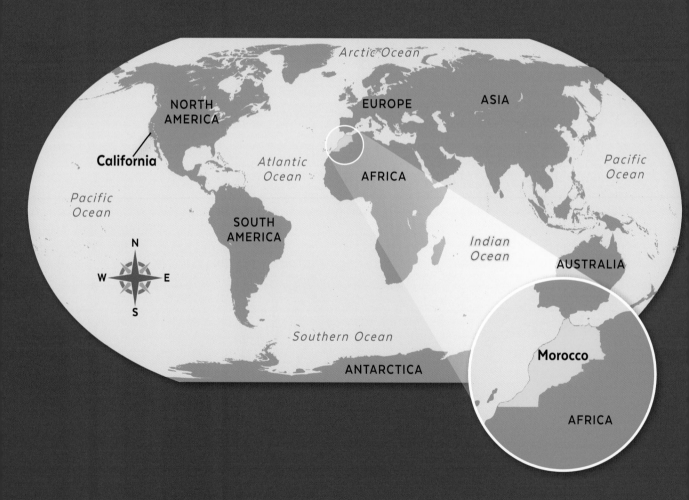

About 34 million people live in Morocco.

Morocco's land is varied.
The country has a long coast and rich **plains**.

Mountains stretch across the middle of Morocco.

Atlas Mountains

The huge Sahara Desert is east of the mountains.

Sahara Desert

The Sahara is the largest hot desert in the world!

What animals live in Morocco?

The desert is home to hopping **rodents** called jerboas.

Big-eyed geckos scurry across the sand.

Goats and camels also live in Morocco. Some goats climb trees to feed on leaves and fruit!

Morocco has a long history.

Two main groups—the Berbers and Arabs—settled the area.

Over the years, power shifted between them.

Berber buildings from the 1600s

In the 1900s, France and Spain controlled the country.

Mohammed VI of Morocco

Today, a king rules Morocco.

Religion is an important part of Moroccan life.

About 98 percent of people are Muslim.

Muslim people practice Islam. They often bow when they pray.

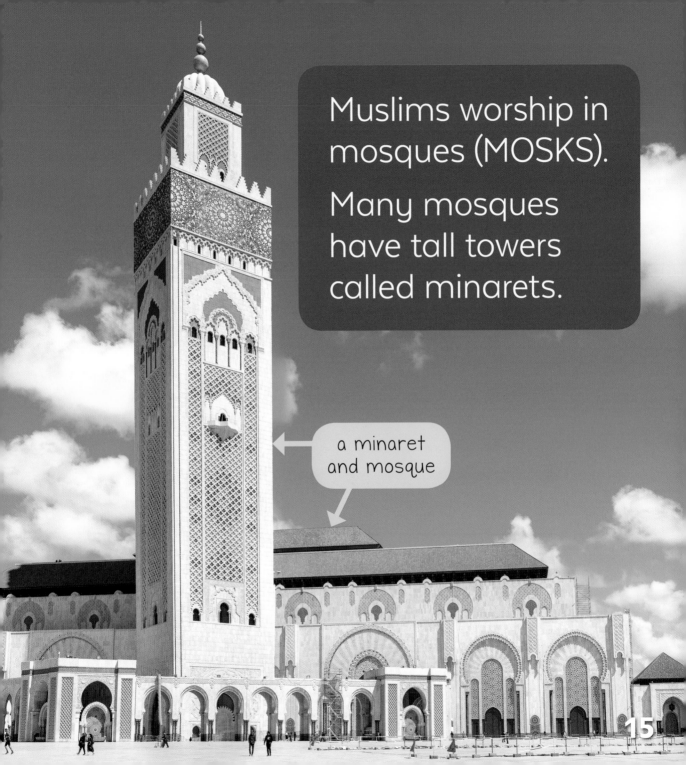

Muslims worship in mosques (MOSKS).

Many mosques have tall towers called minarets.

a minaret and mosque

15

Most Moroccans speak Arabic or Berber.

This is how you say *hello* in Arabic:

Ahlan (ah-LAN)

This is how you say *hello* in Berber:

Azul (ah-ZOOL)

Many Moroccans also speak French.

The **capital** of Morocco is Rabat.

Casablanca is the country's largest city. Over three million people live there!

Most Moroccan cities have big markets called *souks* (SOOKS).

A popular city in Morocco is Marrakech (MAR-uh-kesh).

It's famous for its gardens and markets.

The *medina* is a very old section of the city.

It has winding streets.

a garden in Marrakech

Marrakech dates back to the year 1062!

Moroccan food is full of flavor!

Meats and vegetables are mixed with spices and herbs.

Moroccans love sweet mint tea. The tea is served in small glasses.

Food is often cooked in a *tagine* (tah-JEEN).

A tagine is a clay pot with a tall, skinny top.

23

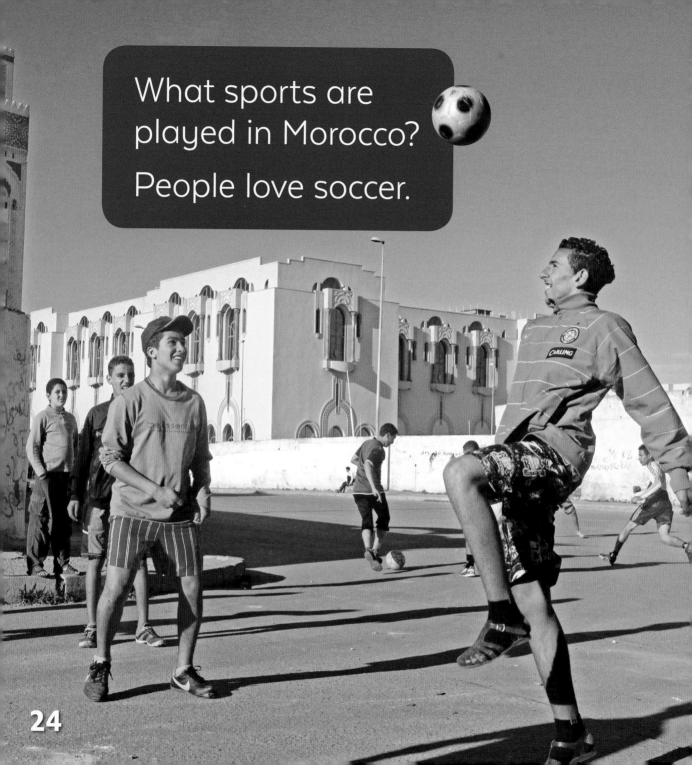

What sports are played in Morocco?
People love soccer.

24

Golf is also a favorite pastime.

Hole in one!

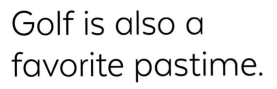

Morocco is home to the Marathon Des Sables. It's a six-day-long race in the Sahara Desert!

Beautiful leather goods come from Morocco.

Workers **dye** leather in big pits.

Then, the leather is made into colorful shoes and bags.

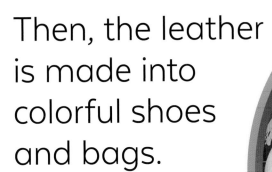

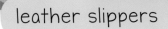
leather slippers

Morocco is also famous for its handmade pottery.

Morocco has over 11 million visitors each year!

People love to visit the desert.

They ride camels over huge sand dunes.

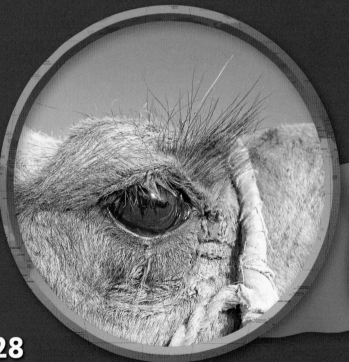

Look at those long lashes! A camel's eyelashes protect its eyes during desert sandstorms.

sand dunes

Capital city: Rabat

Population of Morocco:
About 34 million

Main languages:
Arabic, Berber, and French

Money:
Moroccan dirham

Major religion: Islam

Neighboring country:
Algeria

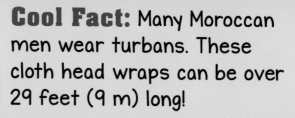

Cool Fact: Many Moroccan men wear turbans. These cloth head wraps can be over 29 feet (9 m) long!

capital (KAP-uh-tuhl) the city where a country's government is based

dye (DYE) to color or stain something

plains (PLAYNZ) large, flat areas of land

rodents (ROH-duhnts) a group of animals with large front teeth that includes rats and mice

Index

Read More

Blauer, Ettagale, and Jason Lauré. *Morocco (Enchantment of the World).* New York: Children's Press (2015).

Simmons, Walter. *Morocco (Exploring Countries).* Minnetonka, MN: Bellwether (2012).

Learn More Online

To learn more about Morocco, visit
www.bearportpublishing.com/CountriesWeComeFrom

About the Author

Joyce Markovics lives in Ossining, New York.
She's written over 100 books for young readers.
Joyce loves to prepare Moroccan mint tea for
her dear friend, Nicole G.